CHANCE
PARTICULARS

CHANCE
PARTICULARS

A Writer's Field Notebook
for Travelers, Bloggers,
Essayists, Memoirists, Novelists,
Journalists, Adventurers, Naturalists,
Sketchers, and Other Note-Takers
and Recorders of Life

SARA MANSFIELD TABER

ILLUSTRATED BY MAUD TABER-THOMAS

Johns Hopkins University Press
Baltimore

Johns Hopkins University Press
2715 North Charles Street
Baltimore, Maryland 21218-4363
www.press.jhu.edu

Library of Congress Cataloging-in-Publication Data

Names: Taber, Sara Mansfield, author.
Title: Chance particulars : a writer's field notebook for travelers,
    bloggers, essayists, memoirists, novelists, journalists, adventurers,
    naturalists, sketchers, and other note-takers and recorders of life /
    Sara Mansfield Taber.
Description: Baltimore, Maryland : Johns Hopkins University Press, 2018.
Identifiers: LCCN 2017033306 | ISBN 9781421425085 (pbk. : alk. paper) |
    ISBN 9781421425092 (electronic) | ISBN 1421425084 (pbk. : alk. paper) |
    ISBN 1421425092 (electronic)
Subjects: LCSH: Authorship—Handbooks, manuals, etc.
Classification: LCC PN147 .T31 2018 | DDC 808.02—dc23
LC record available at https://lccn.loc.gov/2017033306

A catalog record for this book is available from the British Library.

Special discounts are available for bulk purchases of this book. For more information, please contact Special Sales at 410-516-6936 or specialsales@press.jhu.edu.

Johns Hopkins University Press uses environmentally friendly book materials, including recycled text paper that is composed of at least 30 percent post-consumer waste, whenever possible.

Cover and book design by Kimberly Glyder

FOR PETER, MAUD, AND FORREST
AND FOR THOSE WITH A YEN TO NOTE
LIFE'S EVENTS AND OCCURRENCES,
COMMON AND UNCOMMON

Let a man get up and say, Behold, this is the truth, and instantly I perceive a sandy
cat filching a piece of fish in the background. Look, you have forgotten the cat, I say.
Nothing has really happened until it has been recorded.

–VIRGINIA WOOLF

Transferring experience from the vat of life into the vessel of the journal is a distillation:
it sieves, concentrates, and ferments. If after many seasons we develop some mastery
of the process, the stuff can become as clear and fiery as brandy.

–HANNAH HINCHMAN

CONTENTS

CHANCE
PARTICULARS

INTRODUCTION

Alastair Reid, in *Whereabouts: Notes on Being a Foreigner*, describes the zest of the traveler on arrival in a new country:

> In a foreign country, the pattern of days is less predictable—each one has its character, and is easier to remember. So, too, the weather; and so, too, the shape and feel of newspapers, the sound of bells, the taste of beer and bread. It is all rather like waking up and not knowing who or where one is. . . . Quite ordinary things take on an edge; one keeps discovering oneself miraculously alive.

The goal of the writer—whether traveler, memoirist, journalist, novelist, or one who keeps a log just for himself—is to live with the keenness of the foreigner, to experience, wide-eyed, the sensations aroused and the events offered up by his peculiar surrounds and then to evoke them so brightly on the page that the reader, too, experiences the foreigner's frisson: discovers him- or herself invigorated, transported to another full and miraculous life. A time-honored way this may be accomplished is through the keeping of a field notebook: through the faithful recording of the this-and-that of life; the atmospheres and incidents; the bells, the beer, the bread.

For many years I have welcomed adults into my writing seminars—wonderful people writing of their travels, their explorations of cattlemen or the KGB, their childhoods, their fictional characters, their complex, rich lives. Often they arrive with bundles of journals and letters, sheaves of collected writings, and rubber-banded stacks of torn envelopes and newspaper corners scribbled with notes they want to turn into vivid memoirs, essays, travel pieces, literary journalism, or stories. Each and every person who enters my room has unique tales to tell and wisdom to impart.

The one thing they too often lack is adequate notes on the very people and places they want to write about. Their notes—and consequently their writings (at least initially)—have a fundamental flaw: an insufficiency of concrete and sensory detail with which to build flavorful, satisfying stories. They haven't made notes at the level of precision that causes a time, place, scene, person, or emotion to quicken on the page. They lack sufficient rich description in their field notebooks—whether those "notebooks" be index cards, computer files, paper-clipped scraps of jottings, or classic black books.

When traveling, gathering bits of the past for a memoir, assembling material for a novel or reportage, or keeping a journal or blog, it is difficult to hold in the mind the many aspects of an experience to record—the very details that would make the experience come to life on the page. I have composed this "field notebook for field notebook keepers" to rectify the situation—to ensure that the holder will keep a notebook so bountiful that the writing, and the essays and stories that may later come from the jottings, will fall off the page like ripe plums.

To me, the two words *field notebook* are among the most romantic in the language. They conjure: Charles Darwin hunching on Galápagoan rocks describing finches; Margaret Mead filling a book with the antics of Samoan girls; Virginia Woolf penning her diary after a day's tramp through the downs; George Orwell huddled in a Barcelona café reporting on the Spanish Civil War.

Muddy-boot biologists, mosquito-slapping naturalists, war reporters, diarists, novelists, voyagers, literary journalists, urban bloggers, ethnographers, and myriad other explorers and watchers—I can see them all clearly in my mind's eye, jotting *in situ* their observations of the world. What these varied scribblers all have in common is the impulse and the need to keep bright notes on life's offerings—to keep a field notebook.

To take time in the midst of, or at the conclusion of, a long day of immersion, to set down that experience in ink in a notebook, is the writer's primary and most basic method for capturing and recording the stuff of life. The proper keeping of a field notebook is key. To me, it is not only one of life's chief joys but a sacred practice.

Besides its practical and romantic purpose—to trap in print that Monarch butterfly that is life on the page—the words *field notebook* also connote hard work. I know the labor well from my own anthropological and literary journalistic field researches for books on the lives of people in Argentina and France, as well as from my forays into memoir and essay. The discipline and devotion required to plunk oneself down at the end of a day of interviewing, hanging out with shepherds, observing the effects of war, or visiting friends to inscribe in ink for all time those events is not to be belittled.

The first field notebook I ever kept was for a field study of Patagonian right whales, my second for a study of Argentine sheep ranchers, and, hooked, I have kept up the practice since, for sundry other writing endeavors.

The practice of the field notebook was, to me, a revelation, as portable paint and easel must have been for the nineteenth-century discoverers of painting *en plein air*. It was also a revolution—a way to grab the spindly leg of life as it flickered by and pin it forever to the page. More, it was a way to live—and to savor that lived life. It offered the chance to live life thrice—at the point of experience, at the point of note-taking, and at the point of reviewing the observations and setting them into a structured tale. Think of the field notebook as a writer's sketchbook.

But why the need for this book: a field notebook for field-notebook keepers? Isn't note-taking an obvious, easy sort of thing—one we all mastered in high school if not before? No, it is not at all easy, especially not to do well.

I have experienced its failings myself. I arrived home from my first year and a half in Patagonia, for instance, having not recorded a single conversation with the ranchers I afterward yearned to write about. I was granted the opportunity of returning to right this negligence and to undertake systematic fieldwork, but such luck is rare. Years later, this time with memoir-writing in mind, when I went to my carton-filled basement to excavate my supposedly rich archive of youthful journals, I had a similar shock: there was nothing in those pages and pages of pennings worth using in a sentence, much less in a book-length memoir. Most of the writing was generalizing and caterwauling on the page. (This is not to belittle the emotional benefit of journal-as-release, but it's advantageous, for the writerly sort, if the journal can serve simultaneously another fruitful purpose.) In my diaries there was no mention of the croquettes eaten or account of the intense conversations my friend Ali and I had about how to catch a boy—the specifics that might have brought those eighth-grade years back in full color. The truth is, it is rare for untutored journal writers and travelers to actually record more than generalities like "Had a delicious meal last night with James and Charlotte," or "The countryside was beautiful." Most record-keepers forget the very details—the beef stew with pickles, the bounding yellow fields of rape, the encounter with a gypsy, the ponderings about beauty—that would cause the experience to live in the reader's mind.

In her beloved novel *Out of Africa* Isak Dinesen evoked for all time the beautiful landscape and wise Kikuyu people of Kenya. Here she recreates an encounter she had after a flight with her friend Denys Finch-Hatton:

Once, when Denys and I had been up, and were landing on the plain of the farm, a very old Kikuyu came up and talked to us:

"You were very high to-day," he said, "we could not see you, only hear the airplane sing like a bee."

I agreed that we had been up high.

"Did you see God?" he asked.

"No, Ndwetti," I said, "we did not see God."

"Aha, then you were not up high enough," he said, "but now tell me: do you think that you will be able to get up high enough to see him?"

"I do not know, Ndwetti," I said.

"And you, Bedâr," he said, turning to Denys, "what do you think? Will you get up high enough in your aeroplane to see God?"

"Really I do not know," said Denys.

"Then," said Ndwetti, "I do not know at all why you two go on flying."

And here, M. F. K. Fisher, inveterate traveler and gourmande extraordinaire, sets before the reader, in *The Gastronomical Me*, a buffet of the meals she enjoyed during a 1936 voyage on a Dutch passenger-freighter:

I don't remember much about the food, except that it was very different from the almost lavish cuisine of the other freighter we knew, the Italian one. It was dull, good, heavy food, but there were many vegetables and salads all the way to England. The coffee was fine, and this time we could afford to drink Dutch beer when we wanted it, and quite a lot of delicate Rhine wine.

The baker had a fight with the chef soon after we left port, and the barber took over all the pastry making . . . or so we heard. We had cake twice a day, in many different shapes but always the same. It was almost like cold omelet, as if it were made of hundreds of egg yolks stirred with a lot of sugar and a little flour and then baked. It was usually in thin solid pieces, like small bricks, elaborately topped with glacéed fruits and always served with flavored whipped cream.

We often had a thick green soup, in the colder seas, filled with cabbage and potatoes and leeks and always with slices of link-sausage floating in it.

And there was one unattractive but delicious thing, a kind of sludge of different vegetables flavored with ham, which the waiter called Udgie-pudgie. I finally saw on a menu that it was Hodgepodge. The captain said the crew loved it, and it was indeed good, in a simple crude way that might offend or bore sophisticated palates.

What if Isak Dinesen had simply written, "Met an old Kikuyu"? and if M. F. K. Fisher had simply noted, "The food was variable onboard ship"?

I have assembled this manual so that, when you are writing in your diary, or dashing off sentences in your travel journal, or recording your field notes for your book of literary journalism, or composing your blog or memoir or novel, you will have a ready reference that will prompt you to record the kinds of details and observations and stories that make for evocative records and tales of life. So that you will summon the sensory detail you need; record the conversations, gestures, and habits of the people you meet; and describe the land with such richness that the people and places you are trying so valiantly to capture spring from the page. And so that, later, when you return to your notes in order to reexperience those times or to turn them into finished pieces of writing, you will have there, in your notebook, the very accounts and stories and details you need and will only have to pluck and arrange.

In this book I set forth lists of all the kinds of material to record while you are traveling or gathering material, while you are blog- or journal-keeping or assembling your (memoir-writing) trip back in time: so that you will not omit some vital aspect and kick yourself later, as I so often have. You will inevitably forget some choice tidbits, but I intend, through the use of this guide, to shorten the list of the forgotten.

When I set out on my large, sprawling book-writing projects—my immersion in the lives of the sheep ranchers of Patagonia and my inquiry into the making of a French village bread loaf—compulsive that I am, I compiled a two-inch, three-ring binder's worth of questionnaires and lists of the aspects of life I wanted to ask about—from inventories of household goods and mental health protocols to queries about money, friendship, and my informants' philosophies of life. I made lists of the kinds of observations I wanted to make of the landscape, street interactions, meals eaten. . . . Over time I threw out the formal questionnaires and boiled my list down to just the sorts of details that could, when later reread at home base, lend themselves to the re-creation and recollection of a people and place. I offer the revised list to the reader here. Despite the deletions, the list still casts a wide net, and its suggestions may seem simple or obvious. When it gets to the actual work in the field, however, it is not so easy to remember to take the time to describe the teacup your sea captain drank from as he recounted his shipwreck in the Falkland Islands—and that teacup may end up the vital metaphor for the entire piece. You never quite know ahead of time what form your final piece of writing will take, so as much detail as you can get down in the field will be money in the bank. I guarantee you will never regret a single extra jotting you made. Instead, you will gloat over your treasures.

I've conceived this guide to be useful for any kind of writing from life: for those, such as voyagers or travel essayists, traveling through a place; for those, like literary journalists, who immerse themselves in a place and systematically collect interview and observational material; for bloggers and diarists; for those working from memory; or for novelists wishing to summon a real place to the page. The book may be a useful reminder to any who strive to recreate a time and place, create vivid portraits, keep a record of their own life's events, or paint a picture of a particular landscape or culture or locale.

There are many fine writing guides that instruct the reader about how to describe a landscape, fashion a portrait, and craft a scene. What this book offers is the assurance that you will have the material with which to write those memorable descriptions, portraits, and scenes. I see this as an old-fashioned handbook or primer, a reminder in the form of lists of what to take notes on while wandering and sojourning in new spots, while reflecting on your life, and while composing and recreating a time, a set of people, and a place. Given that each project is unique, I invite you to add to and personalize this list using the space I have left for that purpose.

The book begins with a review of the elements of fine writing, a reminder, through an example of lively prose, of what it is built of. Then follow eleven sections, each of which spotlights a different kind of material that may be included in a field notebook and that, when accumulated, may yield a satisfying, rich, and thorough coverage of life experience.

PURPOSE OF THE NOTEBOOK

Here, I invite you to set down your initial aims and questions—practical, personal, and intellectual—as you take up your field notebook.

CHANCE PARTICULARS

In this section I urge you to attend to, and make note of, your sensory impressions and record concrete

details of your world with specificity and precision. This practice, applied across all the kinds of material I suggest you collect, makes writing shine.

PLACE

I list in this section the many aspects of place you may wish to record, from landscape and botany to architectural features and street scenes.

PEOPLE

Here is where I direct you to put in print your interviewees' gestures and hairpins along with their conversation, and I urge you to take the time to jot down chance encounters with firemen, bakers, and artists, as well as to make note of your own activities.

FACTS, HISTORY, AND CULTURE

In this section I prompt you to gather the basic information that undergirds your story: population, historical events, sociology, and other background. In addition I suggest that you get on paper your noticings about how people in this particular culture (even if it is your own) eat pie or greet one another.

TECHNICAL AND OTHER PERTINENT INFORMATION

Here I suggest that you record the procedures for curing warts or producing newspapers—whatever may be germane to your interests and objectives.

CHRONICLE

I urge you, in this section, to get down the incidents of ordinary daily life and the inviting aroma of those artichoke tarts you grab when hunger strikes, as well as the names of the fleabag or luxurious hotels you may stay in while traveling.

PERSONAL RESPONSES

The recording of personal, emotional responses to events is a critical part of any field notebook. I advocate that you capture them here. They are what make the record truly yours—unique and authentic.

COMMONPLACE NOTES

This section serves as a reminder to register perspectives and quotations from scholars and experts in your field of interest and to copy down lines from writers you love. Make notes, too, as you visit museums and wander alleys to capture the omnivorous noticings of your peculiar mind. Any of these may well come in handy and stir your own reflections or provide bolstering evidence or the perfect fillip, when, at long last, you read your notebook to mine its wisdom or when you seek to compose a finished work through the harvest of your notebook.

ASSOCIATIONS AND FIGURATIVE LANGUAGE

In this section I invite you to release your mind, like a horse from the paddock, and allow your imagination to gallop and play. Let the associations fly in metaphors that allow your prose, like Pegasus, to take wing.

REFLECTIONS

Finally, not to be forgotten are your intellectual reactions to your experiences.

Just as important as the observations and interactions themselves are the thoughts and reflections you have in response to them.

To conclude the book, I supply, in "Writing Notes," a list of key elements of the writer's craft as an easy reminder while you write your field notes and construct drafts of essays, blog posts, memoirs, journalism, and so forth on their basis. There, as a handy reference, I list the building blocks of elegant writing, the tools of the trade.

A NOTE ON THE COMPOSITION OF THE SECTIONS OF THE BOOK

Each section opens with an excerpt that pertains to its particular focus. For instance, the passage for the section "Purpose of the Notebook" comes from Henry David Thoreau's *Walden*. It is meant to exemplify the sorts of ponderings and motives that may propel a person to keep a field notebook and to show how, if recorded, they may find their way into text. The opening passages in each section are designed to stir the reader's imagination and nourish the inclination to make similar recordings.

I have selected the excerpts from significant literary nonfiction—travel pieces, books of literary journalism, memoirs, diaries, letters, and so on— to provide you with examples of fine landscape description, characterization, or dialogue, which may spur you to write your own. Obviously, I have not been able to be comprehensive as I intend this book to be compact, but I hope to have provided sufficient citation to inspire. I have selected a mixture of classics and more recent work, work of women and men writers, and writings from both far and near.

Following the opening quote for each section, I point to the literary strengths of the chosen passage and then offer a practical list of the kinds of notes to take, as well as a set of directions for doing so, so that you may amass material on the wide array of aspects of experience: for instance, impressions of people and places, details of your daily life, and notes on local history. In the "People" section, for example, I ask you to make notes on an individual's physical appearance, voice, gestures, quirks, habits, passions, and so forth, so that you may assemble the makings of a full and rounded portrait.

The book may be read through from cover to cover, or it may be used as a reference while recording field notes. I have designed it, most particularly, for the latter purpose. My vision is this: of an evening in Provence or Tibet, or at home while settling in to work on a field notebook or journal or memoir, or while sketching in a field or tapping in a blog, the possessor will think to her- or himself, *Hmm . . . I have described the hotel and the street in Lhasa . . .* or *I have written about Peterkin's Drugs back home in Omaha . . . Now what else do I need to make sure to describe?* And

he or she will open this small book and be prompted to record, too, the stink of the butcher shop down the street or the playground on the square where drunken Uncle Jim threw up.

In *A Book of One's Own: People and Their Diaries* Thomas Mallon points to the great boon that may result if you collect in your notebook your own unique details and observations. Here he issues a warning to David Gascoyne, the writer whose Paris journal he is in the course of discussing:

> Just look back to May 13:
> Last night we sat alone in the Place Dauphine, under chestnut trees. It was so warm, the sky so blue and clear. A perfect May night. (Even the *pissoir* nearby sounded like a fountain playing in an Italian piazza!) The white steps of the Palais de Justice glimmered like a more romantic balustrade in the background.—We were silent most of the time. Some people went by with their dog. We were there for perhaps an hour. I shall never forget it.
>
> You certainly seem to have forgotten it by September. It's a good thing you'll have this book to bring it back to you. Anyone who's sat in that little square can tell you it's still just like that—the benches, the chestnut trees, the white steps. But someone else's reminders won't do. Someone else's chestnut trees aren't your chestnut trees; and his white steps aren't yours, either. You want the ones you had on May 13, 1938. Above all you want

the detail of that dog going by, and the jokey way you were struck by the pissoir—chance particulars that will really let it come back to you, that will let you open the diary forty, fifty years later and hear it playing your song.

It is those "chance particulars" that I hope this field notebook for field-note-book keepers will help you to catch, so that your writing—whether travel account, novel, journal, blog, literary journalism, or memoir—will play your own rare song.

ELEMENTS OF
FINE WRITING

Before embarking on the field notebook proper, it is useful to review the features of elegant writing. Here is an episode from Bruce Chatwin's book of travels, *In Patagonia*, an example of fine prose assembled from field notes:

> I took the night bus on to the Chubut Valley. By next morning I was in the village of Gaimán, the centre of Welsh Patagonia today. The valley was about five miles wide, a net of irrigated fields and poplar windbreaks, set between the white cliffs of the barancas—a Nile Valley in miniature.
>
> The older houses in Gaimán were of red brick, with sash windows and neat vegetable gardens and ivy trained to grow over the porches. The name of one house was Nith-y-dryw, the Wren's Nest. Inside, the rooms were whitewashed and had brown painted doors, polished brass handles and grandfather clocks. The colonists came with few possessions but they clung to their family clocks.
>
> Mrs. Jones's teashop lay at the far end of the village where the bridge crossed over to the Bethel. Her plums were ripe and her garden full of roses.
>
> "I can't move, my dear," she called through. "You'll have to come and talk to me in the kitchen."
>
> She was a squat old lady in her eighties. She sat propped up at a scrubbed deal table filling lemon-curd tarts.
>
> "I can't move an inch, my darling. I'm crippled. I've had the arthritis since the flood and have to be carried everywhere."
>
> Mrs. Jones pointed to the line where the floodwater came, above the blue-painted dado, on the kitchen wall. "Stuck in here I was, with the water up to my neck."
>
> She came out nearly sixty years ago from Bangor in North Wales. She had not left the valley since. She remembered a family I knew in Bangor and said: "Fancy, it's a small world."

"You won't believe it," she said. "Not to look at me now you won't. But I was a beauty in my day." And she talked about a laddie from Manchester and his bouquet of flowers and the quarrel and the parting and the ship.

"'And how are the morals back home?" she asked. "Down?"

"Down."

"And they're down here too. All this killing. You can't tell where it'll end."

Mrs. Jones's grandson helped run the teashop. He ate too much cake for his own good. He called his grandmother "Granny" but otherwise he did not speak English or Welsh.

I slept in the Draigoch Guest House. It was owned by Italians who played Neapolitan songs on the juke box late into the night.

Perusal of this brief passage from Chatwin's book reveals some of the ingredients that make this author's writing a pleasure to read.

USE OF THE SENSES

Chatwin calls on all the senses to evoke his experience of a particular person and place, in this case Mrs. Jones's Patagonian teashop: sight (*red brick, ivy, grandfather clocks*); taste (*plums, cake, lemon-curd tarts*); smell (*roses*); touch (*polished brass handles, floodwater*); sound (*Neapolitan songs*).

SPECIFICITY AND CONCRETE DETAIL

Notice how Chatwin selects a few tangible details that summon a picture of the Patagonian village. He takes care to record the actual name of one of the dwellings and includes description of both the interior and exterior of the house to which he pays a visit:

> The older houses in Gaimán were of red brick, with sash windows and neat vegetable gardens and ivy trained to grow over the porches. The name of one house was *Nith-y-dryw*, the Wren's Nest. Inside, the rooms were whitewashed and had brown painted doors, polished brass handles and grandfather clocks.

QUALITY OF LANGUAGE

Check the rhythm, phrasing, and lengths of Chatwin's sentences. Observe his syntax, word choice, and use of alliteration:

> Mrs. Jones's teashop lay at the far end of the village where the bridge crossed over to the Bethel. Her plums were ripe and her garden full of roses.

FIGURATIVE LANGUAGE

Note how Chatwin uses simile, metaphor, and symbol to enrich his work. The town was "a Nile Valley in miniature," the dwellings, by implication, were like wrens' nests.

UNIQUE VOICE

Chatwin harnesses his own particular sensibility and personality, his own peculiar observations, accents, phrasings, thoughts, and judgments in the expression of his unique voice:

> Mrs. Jones's grandson helped run the teashop. He ate too much cake for his

own good. He called his grandmother "Granny" but otherwise he did not speak English or Welsh.

SENSE OF PLACE

In a very few sentences the writer offers a rich sense of place, from the inner chambers already mentioned to the hawk's-eye view:

> The valley was about five miles wide, a net of irrigated fields and poplar windbreaks, set between the white cliffs of the barancas.

INTERESTING, MULTI-FACETED CHARACTERS

Chatwin captures Mrs. Jones's sweetness, industriousness, and no-nonsense forthrightness in his description of her. Note how the dialogue, especially, brings the Welsh woman to life:

> "I can't move, my dear," she called through. "You'll have to come and talk to me in the kitchen."
>
> She was a squat old lady in her eighties. She sat propped up at a scrubbed deal table filling lemon-curd tarts.
>
> "I can't move an inch, my darling. I'm crippled. I've had the arthritis since the flood and have to be carried everywhere."
>
> Mrs. Jones pointed to the line where the floodwater came, above the blue-painted dado, on the kitchen wall.
>
> "Stuck in here I was, with the water up to my neck."

MEMORABLE SCENES

In a short scene Chatwin captures an individual's experience of a violent era in Argentine history:

> ". . . All this killing. You can't tell where it'll end."

LIKABLE NARRATOR

Via just one word, the word "down," in the following dialogue, Chatwin shows the reader his rapport with his informant:

> "And how are the morals back home?" she asked. "Down?"
>
> "Down."
>
> "And they're down here too . . ."

Through this and by way of the empathic and sensitive choices he makes in characterization, he establishes himself as an appealing and interesting guide, a narrator whose viewpoints both entertain and inspire the reader's identification and interest.

COMPELLING SENSE OF STORY

In this tiny section from his chronicle Chatwin both offers up a ministory of a transplanted Welsh woman and whets the reader's appetite for the next entry. In a few words he simultaneously pins the turning point in the Welsh woman's youth:

> "You won't believe it," she said. "Not to look at me now you won't. But I was a beauty in my day." And she talked about a laddie from Manchester and his bouquet of flowers and the quarrel and the parting and the ship.

VIVID, THOUGHT-PROVOKING EXPLORATION OF A PLACE, QUESTION, THEME

In this episode Chatwin gives the reader a sip of what it means to be a Welsh immigrant in "the village of Gaimán, the centre of Welsh Patagonia today."

FASCINATING FACTS (HISTORY, SOCIOLOGY, CULTURE, POLITICS, ART . . .)

In the same section, Chatwin provides a sense of the history of the Welsh immigrants and their isolation:

> I took the night bus on to the Chubut Valley. By next morning I was in the village of Gaimán, the centre of Welsh Patagonia today. . . . She came out nearly sixty years ago from Bangor in North Wales. She had not left the valley since. She remembered a family I knew in Bangor and said: "Fancy, it's a small world."

INTRIGUING INSIGHTS AND REFLECTIONS

Chatwin seizes one treasured object as a metaphor for the Patagonian Welsh and their values:

> The colonists came with few possessions but they clung to their family clocks.

HONESTY AND IDIOSYNCRASY

In the final sentence of this episode Chatwin lets the reader in on his wide-ranging tastes: his appreciation for high-spirited young men who live in the moment, as well as aged, hard-working, time-conscious Welsh women. One can imagine him, saturated with lemon tarts, afterward singing arm-in-arm with the young Italians:

> I slept in the Draigoch Guest House. It was owned by Italians who played Neapolitan songs on the juke box late into the night.

ELEMENTS OF FINE WRITING

As you write up your field notes, try to keep in mind these aspects of strong prose:

Use of the Senses

Specificity and Concrete Detail

Quality of Language:

> word choice
> phrasing
> rhythm
> sentence length
> syntax
> alliteration

Figurative Language:

> simile and metaphor

Unique Voice

Sense of Place

Interesting, Multi-faceted Characters

Memorable Scenes

Likable Narrator

Compelling Sense of Story

Vivid, Thought-Provoking Exploration
   of a Place, Question, Theme

Fascinating Facts

Intriguing Insights and Reflections

Honesty and Idiosyncrasy

PURPOSE OF THE NOTEBOOK

Naturalist Henry David Thoreau planted himself in the forest of Concord, Massachusetts, and recorded his experiences and thoughts in the American classic *Walden:*

> I went to the woods because I wished to live deliberately, to front only the essential facts of life, and see if I could not learn what it had to teach, and not, when I came to die, discover that I had not lived.

Thoreau kept his famous journal, as he says, in order to live "deliberately." To live deeply, richly, maximally is perhaps the reason, at its most basic, that any of us keeps a log, but there are as many purposes for keeping a field notebook as there are human beings. Indeed, one human being may have multiple aims in writing. Essayist and memoirist Terry Tempest Williams listed more than seventy reasons in her little essay on the subject—from "I write as a witness to what I have seen," to "I write because you can play on the page like a child left alone in sand," to "I write out of my nightmares and into my dreams."

In *The Shadow of the Sun* journalist Ryszard Kapuscinski described the focus of his collage-portrait of Africa—a book drawn from years of field notes—this way:

> I lived in Africa over several years. . . . I traveled extensively, avoiding official routes, palaces, important personages, and high-level politics. Instead I opted to hitch rides on passing trucks, wander with nomads through the desert, be the guest of peasants of the tropical savannah. . . . This is therefore not a book about Africa, but rather about some people from there—about encounters with them, and time spent together.

Literary journalist Ronald Blythe collected the life stories and outlooks of all the residents of an English village in a group portrait. He noted at the beginning of *Akenfield,* "This book is the quest for the voice of Akenfield, Suffolk, as it sounded during the summer and autumn of 1967."

Novelist and poet Michael Ondaatje described the propulsion for his memoir *Running in the Family*—another book composed of various kinds of field note-taking—as "running to Asia":

> But it was only in the midst of this party among my closest friends, that I realized I would be traveling back to the family I had grown from—those relations from my parents' generation who stood in my memory like frozen opera. I wanted to touch them into words. . . . In my mid-thirties I realized I had slipped past a childhood I had ignored and not understood.

Travel writer Jan Morris wrote in her memoir *Pleasures of a Tangled Life:*

> I told an acquaintance of mine that I was writing a book about Pleasure. . . . I am merely out to show once more, by the examples of my own life and taste, out of my peculiar circumstances, what a pleasure pleasures are. . . .
>
> They include, indeed, many pleasures ordinary enough, pleasures generic and particular, of place and of fancy, sustained and momentary pleasures, pleasures tart and pleasures rather sickly, pleasures of eating, reading, listening to music and being Welsh.

> . . . I can pin it down to specific emotions, of the pleasure that the world in general gives me in the second half of my life; pleasure which, like my life itself, seems to be at bottom a yearning for unity—"the desire and pursuit of the whole."

This "pursuit of the whole" is a common impetus behind notebook-keeping. In her essay "A Sketch of the Past," novelist Virginia Woolf wrote that "the shock-receiving capacity is what makes me a writer." In the essay she elaborates:

> A shock is at once in my case followed by the desire to explain it. I feel that I have had a blow; but it is not, as I thought as a child, simply a blow from an enemy hidden behind the cotton wool of daily life; it is or will become a revelation of some order; it is a token of some real thing behind appearances; and I make it real by putting it into words. It is only by putting it into words that I make it whole; this wholeness means that it has lost its power to hurt me; it gives me, perhaps because by doing so I take away the pain, a great delight to put the severed parts together. Perhaps this is the strongest pleasure known to me.

Sculptor Anne Truitt, too, wrote to find wholeness. In the beginning of *Daybook: The Journal of an Artist,* she recorded that she wrote to find and confirm her artist self. By years of pouring herself into her art, she felt she had become less visible to herself:

This anguish overwhelmed me until, early one morning and quite without emphasis, it occurred to me that I could simply record my life for one year and see what happened. So I bought a brown notebook like the ones in which I made lecture notes in college, chose a special day (the first of a visit to a friend to Arizona), and began to write, sitting up in bed every morning and writing for as long as seemed right. The only limitation I set was to let the artist speak. My hope was that if I did this honestly I would discover how to see myself from a perspective that would render myself whole in my own eyes.

To live deliberately, to witness, to play, to escape nightmares, to follow dreams, to record time spent with foreigners, to create an oral history of a community, to understand one's past, to record one's pleasures, to transform hurts, to make oneself visible, to find wholeness—these are among the multitudinous purposes a person might have for keeping a field notebook. I can imagine many others: the wish to record the birds one sights each day and ponder their place in the universe, to note the stages in the building of a boat, to track a three-week cooking extravaganza, to chronicle the changes in one's grandchildren, to salve a grief, to scribble thoughts that occur while sketching. The reasons for, and benefits of, field notebook-keeping are gloriously infinite.

GOAL, QUEST, STORY

Record here your thoughts and intentions—your goal, quest, and/or story—as you begin your field notebook.

INITIAL GOAL	Set down your aims, desires, and aspirations as you start your field notebook. Perhaps you have a particular story you wish to pursue. Note it here.

STARTING QUESTIONS	List the questions you would like to answer.

PERSONAL QUEST

Make note of the personal insights
you hope to gain by keeping this notebook.
Perhaps there are internal conflicts
or questions you wish to sort out.

HYPOTHESES
AND ASSUMPTIONS

Log your hunches about what you
will discover, your thoughts
and expectations.

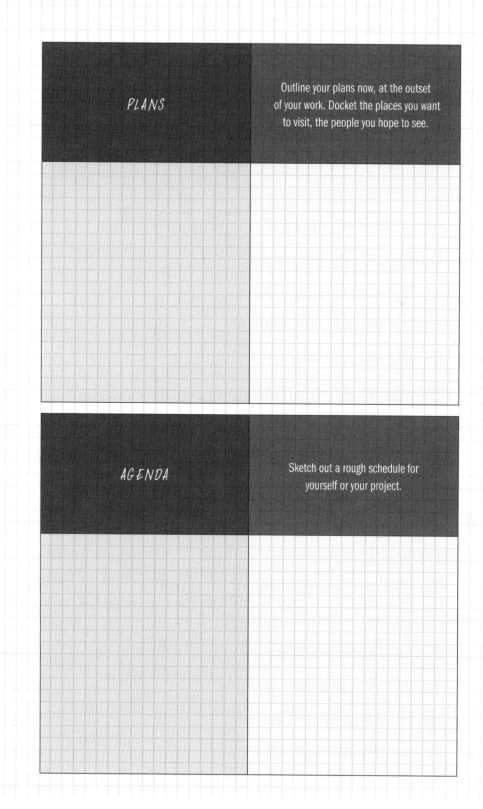

PLANS

Outline your plans now, at the outset of your work. Docket the places you want to visit, the people you hope to see.

AGENDA

Sketch out a rough schedule for yourself or your project.

EVOLUTION IN FOCUS

Record the changes in your focus as your work expands.

REVISED QUESTIONS

Track the new questions that arise as you go deeper into the work.

CHANCE PARTICULARS

Once the notebook is cracked open, the most important rule of thumb for creating a record that sings on the page is to attend to chance particulars—to jot down, in as much detail as possible, the peculiarities of your singular experience. These include the marking down of sensory experiences, as well as the specific, precise details of your world. The setting down of such particulars is the foundation of all strong prose. Pay attention to specificity, precision, and concrete detail, as well as to the use of the senses in the writing of all the kinds of material you may enter into your field notebook. Chance particulars make writing sparkle.

USE OF THE SENSES

Harper Lee describes the fictional town made famous in her book *To Kill a Mockingbird*:

> Maycomb was an old town, but it was a tired old town when I first knew it. In rainy weather the streets turned to red slop; grass grew on the sidewalks, the court-house sagged in the square. Somehow, it was hotter then; a black dog suffered on a summer's day; bony mules hitched to Hoover carts flicked flies in the sweltering shade of the live oaks on the square. Men's stiff collars wilted by nine in the morning. Ladies bathed before noon, after their three o'clock naps, and by nightfall were like soft tea-cakes with frostings of sweat and sweet talcum.
>
> People moved slowly then. They ambled across the square, shuffled in and out of the stores around it, took their time about everything. A day was twenty-four hours long but seemed

longer. There was no hurry, for there was nowhere to go, nothing to buy and no money to buy it with, nothing to see outside the boundaries of Maycomb County. But it was a time of vague optimism for some of the people; Maycomb County had recently been told that it had nothing to fear but fear itself.

In her portrayal of Maycomb, Harper Lee calls up all the senses: sight (*red slop, black dog*); smell (*mules, sweet talcum*); sound (*flicked, shuffled, "nothing to fear but fear itself"*); taste (*tea-cakes*). Most of all she evokes the sense of touch (*slop, sagged, stiff collars, sweat*).

SENSORY IMPRESSIONS

Use your senses to record all you experience:

Smells, Textures, Tastes, Sounds, and Sights

SMELL

Catch on paper the aromas and odors wafting about.

TOUCH

Depict the textures of this place: the feel of the cloth, the succulence of the vegetation, the density of the air.

Evoke the taste of the local bread, coffee, beans . . .

Give words to the late-night sounds, morning noises, birdcalls, car horns, and music you hear.

SIGHT

Paint on the page the predominant colors, face shapes, street scenes of this place.

SPECIFICITY, PRECISION, AND CONCRETE DETAIL

Alfred Kazin serves up his childhood Brooklyn in *A Walker in the City:*

> Walking with my mother to the El at the other end of Sutter Avenue, I would stop under the awning of the remnants store to watch the light falling through the holes in the buttons lining the window, and as we went past Belmont Avenue would stare in hungry pleasure at the fruits and vegetables on the open stands, the cherries glistening with damp as the storekeeper walked under his awning lightly passing a watering can over them; I would smell the sweat on the horses pulling the Italians' watermelon wagons—"Hey you ladies! *Freschi* and good!"; and breathe in the cloying sweetness of the caramels and chocolate syrup in the candy wholesaler's, the fumes of Turkish cigarettes from the "Odessa" and "Roumanian" tearooms, the strange sweetness from the splintered discarded crates where blotches of rotted fruit could still be seen crushed against the nailheads. . . .

> Then home again, to the wet newsprint smell of the first editions of the *News* on the stands and the crackle of the hot dogs in the delicatessen windows—back to the old folks sitting outside our tenement on kitchen chairs, biting into polly seeds and drinking ice water out of milk bottles. Red and blue lights wink untiringly at us from the movie's long electric sign at the other end of Chester Street; the candy stores and delicatessens are ablaze. In the sky a blimp like a feebly smoking cigar floats in from some naval

base along the coast. The dampness of
the summer evening is in the last odors
of all the suppers on the block, the salt
in the air, the voices storming at each
other behind the yellow window shades,
the cries of the boys racing each other
around the block. In a moment of
unbelievable quiet a girl across the way
can be heard stickily trying note on note
from *Für Elise* on an untuned box piano.
The tones buzz against my grateful
brain, gather themselves up into one
swelling wave before they fall into the
theme, then resume like a fly complain-
ing its way up a windowpane.

In addition to evoking many sense
impressions in his depiction of his
hometown, Kazin uses the exact names
of streets, piano music, tearooms,
and newspapers. He also makes very
close, grounded, particular observations—bringing to the reader many
vivid, precise details: damp cherries, a
storekeeper sprinkling a watering can,
watermelon wagons and crates of rotted
fruit "crushed against the nailheads,"
old folks "drinking ice water out of milk
bottles," and "a blimp like a feebly smok-
ing cigar." The combination of sense
impressions, specificity, and precise
detail make Kazin's Brooklyn bustle on
the page.

SPECIFICITY, PRECISION, AND CONCRETE DETAIL

Jot down, with as much exactitude as possible, the distinguishing details of the world around you. Use all your observational powers, bringing to bear the rich perspectives of your partic-ular sensibility, culture, history, and experience. These precise details of your world, specific sights and scenes, will give authority and vivacity to your account.

Strive always to *show* rather than *tell* the reader what you notice. As Kazin *shows* us, through description of "note on note," a girl's painstaking devotion to her piano practice, *show* how people with whom you interact are strong, nurturing, or angry. Seize select incidental details such as those caught by Kazin:

The chants of hawkers
The containers in which fruit is stored
The food sold on the street
Snacks eaten by old people
The look of the sky
Snippets of overheard conversation
Strains of music

In general, make specific, precise note
    of details:

Names of streets, shops, restaurants,
    businesses, woods, mountains, parks
The appearance of people: looks on their
    faces, clothing, gestures, actions, gait,
    what they carry . . .
Storefronts and window displays
Furniture
Placards and printed matter
Foods in the vicinity
Objects that catch your eye
Conversations you hear
Animals on the loose
Trash
Cars on the street
The earth, the sky, the quality of the light

NOTE BELOW SPECIFIC, PRECISE, CONCRETE DETAILS ABOUT THE WORLD AROUND YOU.

NOTE BELOW SPECIFIC, PRECISE, CONCRETE DETAILS ABOUT THE WORLD AROUND YOU.

PLACE

Place is the literal and figurative ground from which good writing sprouts. To encompass all that place is, I encourage you to notice and render in your notebook both natural places—landscape and nature—and constructed ones—towns, streets, and buildings.

LANDSCAPE AND NATURE

Out of Africa is Isak Dinesen's tale of her life on a coffee plantation in Kenya. Here she sets the reader in place:

> I had a farm in Africa, at the foot of the Ngong Hills. The Equator runs across these highlands, a hundred miles to the North, and the farm lay at an altitude of over six thousand feet. In the day-time you felt that you had got high up, near to the sun, but the early mornings and evenings were limpid and restful, and the nights were cold.
>
> The geographical position, and the height of the land combined to create a landscape that had not its like in all the world. There was no fat on it and no luxuriance anywhere; it was Africa distilled up through six thousand feet, like the strong and refined essence of a continent. The colours were dry and burnt, like the colours in pottery. The trees had a light delicate foliage, the structure of which was different from that of the trees in Europe; it did not

grow in bows or cupolas, but in horizontal layers, and the formation gave to the tall solitary trees a likeness to the palms, or a heroic and romantic air like fullrigged ships with their sails clewed up, and to the edge of a wood a strange appearance as if the whole wood were faintly vibrating. Upon the grass of the great plains the cooked bare old thorn-trees were scattered, and the grass was spiced like thyme and bog-myrtle; in some places the scent was so strong, that it smarted in the nostrils. All the flowers that you found on the plains, or upon the creepers and liana in the native forest, were diminutive like flowers of the downs,—only just in the beginning of the long rains a number of big, massive heavy-scented lilies sprang out on the plains. The views were immensely wide. Everything that you saw made for greatness and freedom, unequalled nobility.

Examine Dinesen's iconic illumination of the landscape of Kenya—how she describes the texture of the air (*limpid and restful*) and the barrenness of the earth (*there was no fat on it*). The passage is enhanced by her word choices (*cooked bare old thorn trees*); use of simile (trees *like fullrigged ships . . .*); sparking of the senses (*dry and burnt; spiced like thyme and bog-myrtle; heavy-scented lilies;* and *smarted in the nostrils*); specificity (*creepers and liana*); and idiosyncratic judgments (Africa is *like the refined essence of a continent;* trees have *a heroic and romantic air*).

In the excerpt she touches on the geography of the place, its topography, its flora, and its weathers, all of which land the reader in that dry immensity.

LANDSCAPE AND NATURE

In your field notebook, note:

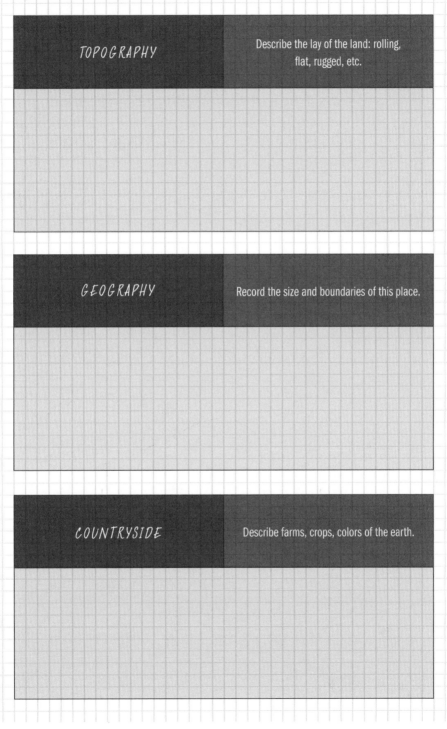

TOPOGRAPHY

Describe the lay of the land: rolling, flat, rugged, etc.

GEOGRAPHY

Record the size and boundaries of this place.

COUNTRYSIDE

Describe farms, crops, colors of the earth.

WEATHER

Observe and record the sunshine, clouds, rainfall, wind.

FLORA

Specify the prevalent types of trees, bushes, flowers, etc.

FAUNA

List the animals that inhabit this place, wild and domestic.

INSECTS

Make note of the mosquitoes, ants, and spiders that dwell here.

BIRD LIFE

Research and jot down names of the local birds.

TOWNS, STREETS, AND BUILDINGS

Ryszard Kapuscinski places the reader in the middle of the capital of Ghana in *The Shadow of the Sun:*

> I've been here for a week. I am trying to get to know Accra. It is like an overgrown small town that has reproduced itself many times over, crawled out of the bush, out of the jungle, and come to a halt at the shores of the Gulf of Guinea. Accra is flat, single-storied, humble, though there are some buildings with two or more floors. No sophisticated architecture, no excess or pomp. Ordinary plaster, pastel-colored walls—pale yellow, pale green. The walls have numerous water stains. Fresh ones. After the rainy season, entire constellations of stains appear, collages, mosaics, fantastical maps, flowery flourishes. The downtown is densely built up. Traffic, crowds, bustle—life takes place out in the street. The street is a roadway delineated on both sides by an open sewer. There are no sidewalks. Cars mingle with the crowds. Everything moves in concert—pedestrians, automobiles, bicycles, carts, cows and goats. On the sides, beyond the sewer, along the entire length of the street, domestic scenes unfold. Women are pounding manioc, baking taro bulbs over the coals, cooking dishes of one sort or another, hawking chewing gum, crackers and aspirin, washing and drying laundry. Right out in the open, as if a decree had been issued commanding everyone to leave his house at eight a.m. and remain in the street. In reality, there is another reason: apartments are small, cramped, stuffy. There is no ventilation, the atmosphere inside is heavy, the smells stale, there is no air to breathe. Besides, spending the day in the street enables one to participate in social life. The women talk nonstop, yell, gesticulate, laugh. Standing over a pot or a washbasin, they have an excellent vantage point. They can see their neighbors, passersby, the entire street; they can listen in on quarrels and gossip, observe accidents. All day long they are among others, in motion, and in the fresh air.

Flat, single-storied, humble; pale yellow, pale green; plaster walls; water stains . . . in *fantastical maps, flowery flourishes*—with these carefully chosen details Kapuscinski transports the reader to the center of Accra, the town that has "crawled out of the bush, out of the jungle, and come to a halt at the shores of the Gulf of Guinea." The journalist uses his deep local knowledge to make comments such as "life takes place out in the street"; then he backs them up with evidence: women pounding manioc, baking taro bulbs, hawking chewing gum, crackers, and aspirin.

TOWNS

Basic layout—grid, concentric, etc. streets—width, names; Shops—names, types; Town hall, library, schools; Restaurants; Churches and temples; Museums; House types; Pace and atmosphere; Street scenes—bustle, colors; Sorts of people—business men, hawkers, etc.

BUILT ENVIRONMENT

Note architectural style, building materials.

COMMERCIAL ENVIRONMENT

List types of businesses, billboards, advertising.
Make notes of look and feel of shops, items bought, interactions with salespeople.

INDOOR SETTINGS

Jot notes on: Furnishings, textures, wall colors and decoration; Cutlery, plates, table cloths; Curios, calendars, photographs, etc.

Effective descriptions of people may include and range from individual portraits and recapitulations of interviews to accounts of random encounters, personal activities, and observations of social life.

PORTRAITS AND INTERVIEWS

John McPhee, literary journalist and master of portraiture, brings to life, in *The Crofter and the Laird,* a resident of the Scottish island of Colonsay:

> Donald Garvard—who is a big and powerful man, with speckled skin and a handsome, weathered face—strides alongside his two dozen beef cattle in a heavy mist on the grasslands of Balaromin Mor, reddish-gray-brown curly hair streaming out behind his knitted cap, a crook in his hand. He looks like an actor, and he talks like one, with a baritone greeting. He removes his cap. There is no hair beneath it. He has the most luxuriant fringe in Scotland.

> Resident in Garvard, he has long since annexed the grazings of Balaromin Mor, and he also works a croft in Kilchattan for an elderly aunt and uncle—in all, some fifteen hundred acres. Donald Garvard is probably the only farmer or crofter in the history of Colonsay who has gone to a public school. . . .

> In a context of individualism, Donald Garvard is particularly individualistic, like his father, Colum Oronsay, who used to stir mayonnaise into his coffee. Donald Garvard sometimes wears shorts, polo shirts, and red slippers. If his feet are cold when he is visiting at someone's house, he will lie down on the floor and stick his legs into the oven. People around the island seem to talk about him more than they do about almost anyone else with the possible exception of the laird and Andrew Oronsay.

> "Donald Garvard is a generous man. He would lend his last hundred pounds."

> "He comes in like a bit of a breeze."

> "He's a hale fellow."

"He has a strong, Highland sense of humor."

"He's a deep thinker, a seeker after truth and knowledge."

"Aye, he has used his education to good purpose intellectually."

"I've had some quite deep philosophic talks with him—I mean, right down to it."

"On the other hand, Donald Garvard can be a bastard, and when Donald Garvard's got a bucket in him, he can be a pest of hell."

"Aye, he likes a tot of whisky."

"When he is halfway over, he is great company."

Notice how McPhee acquaints the reader with Donald Garvard through physical description (*powerful, speckled skin, curly hair streaming out behind his knitted cap*); carefully chosen morsels of personal history (he's *the only crofter who's gone to public school*); peculiarities of habit (*red slippers*, a penchant for *sticking his legs in the oven*); and others' opinions of him. The list of quotes about Garvard give heft and roundness to the reader's sense of him, as well as showing off the rich results of the in-depth interviewing McPhee does in the course of his work as a literary journalist.

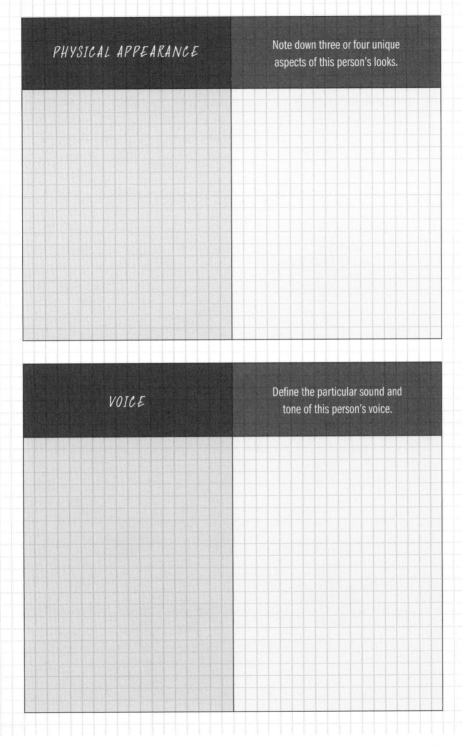

PHYSICAL APPEARANCE

Note down three or four unique aspects of this person's looks.

VOICE

Define the particular sound and tone of this person's voice.

DETAILS OF CHARACTERIZATION

Jot down all the specifics you remember to capture this particular person's sensibility and personality: gestures, clothing, prize possessions, habits, preferences, pet peeves, quirks, passions, etc. What does she eat for breakfast? What does he have in his pockets?

OTHERS' PERSPECTIVES

Catch any comments others might have made about the person.

IMPRESSIONS

Reflect on what sort of person this is:

What is the recipe for being this person?

What does she live for, dream of?

What can he not live without?

What has been her happiest moment,
most important triumph, greatest sadness?

What did this person make
you think, feel, want?

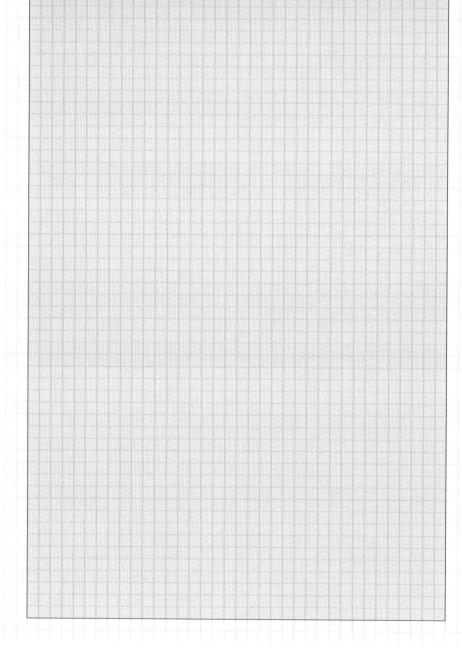

LIST OF QUESTIONS

Register here the basic list of the questions you will be asking interviewees.

RECORD OF INTERVIEW

Register: interview date, name of interviewee, notes. Take notes on the interview, as close to verbatim as possible.

DESCRIPTION OF INTERVIEWEE

Make notes on physical appearance, gestures, voice, dreams, key possessions, core beliefs, and other particulars of character.

INTERVIEW SUMMARY

Write a gist of what this interviewee told you.

Jot down key quotes, repeated phrases or expressions.

Make note of the main points this person wanted to get across.

Note what this person added to your story, what answers he/she provided.

Set down: What was important to him/her

What surprised you

What you learned

How the interview changed your views

What further information you need

INTERVIEW CONTEXT AND OTHER DETAILS

SETTING	Describe the place in which the interview occurred: room size, furniture, key objects, surrounding trees . . .

CONCURRENT ACTIVITIES	Record what you did while talking: what you ate, where you sat, what your informant fiddled with . . .

ENCOUNTERS, OBSERVATIONS, AND ACTIVITIES

In "French Dreams," a chapter of her memoir *Pleasures of a Tangled Life,* Jan Morris sets out episodes from her visits to French towns. Here is a "cameo" of a morning errand:

Finally I record an episode in a small market town in the very center of France, where I stopped one morning to buy myself some toothpaste. Because it was market day, I had to join a queue of people waiting for prescriptions to be filled at the pharmacist's. Through the shop's tinted window the bustle of the market showed the movement of ungainly rib-sided vans, the unrolling of awnings, clothes hanging from racks, heads passing this way and that, and I could hear shouting sometimes, and the revving of engines.

Inside everything was different. Like all French pharmacies, the shop was austerely up-to-date. There were electronic devices of several kinds behind the counter, all gray and white, with paper scrolling out of printers, and a computer screen greenish in a corner. The filing system was of gray steel, its drawers moving on almost silent rollers. Not a bottle could be seen. On the counter there were only one or two displays of shampoos and medicinal soaps, dummies I suspect. The atmosphere was hushed, and the line of customers, mostly elderly and well wrapped up, waited in silence as though to show respect for all this technique.

Behind the counter, the young pharmacist and his wife, both in white coats, were quietly preparing medicines, summoning data from disks, checking the computer screen, rolling those soundless drawers. It seemed almost a betrayal of the times, when they had to wrap a box of pills in perfectly ordinary paper, even though they did seal it with deft manipulations of Scotch tape from a dispenser. They talked to their customers in undertones, and the clients in turn accepted their medicines with murmured thanks and walked quietly away, sometimes nodding a greeting, no more, to acquaintances in the queue. Whenever the shop door was opened it allowed inside, for a moment or two, a sudden clash of noises, smells and colors from the market.

Well after nine-thirty, the pharmacist's assistant arrived, flustered because she was late. The queue eyed her as she hurried by. She took off her raincoat, hanging it in a cupboard, put on a white overall, tidied her hair hastily in a mirror, and joined her employers at the prescription counter. As she did so the pharmacist, moving to the other end of the counter, quite deliberately bumped her with his elbow. Everybody saw it. All the women in the queue took note of it. The pharmacist's wife saw it. There was nothing furtive about it. It was an open, calculated bump. It seemed to me like a message, to which everyone but me was privy. The assistant, I noticed, looked rather surly as she took the impact. The pharmacist's wife stared stony-faced, first at her husband, then at the girl. The silence of the customers became a watchful, waiting silence, but nothing more happened, and soon the assistant too was busily checking, calculating and expertly detaching strips of adhesive tape.

What could it mean? Were the pharmacist and his assistant having an affair? Was his passion of the night before the cause of her lateness in the morning? The bump might have been a nudge, an acknowledgement of past delights, a hint of lusts to come. If so, then the wife must surely be complicit to the liaison, and so also must many of the customers—who must have known, I felt sure, not only the assistant, but the boss himself, and his cool, contemporary, self-controlled, probably Paris-educated wife since they were children. Ah, I thought to myself, the flying of time, the old stories!

But on the other hand perhaps they particularly disliked each other, the chemist and his assistant? The bump might just as easily have been a vicious little blow, intended to hurt. The wife's glance might have been saying yes, quite right, the idle little bitch, you show her! When my turn came to reach the counter it was the assistant who chanced to serve me, but her eyes told me nothing as she handed me my toothpaste, and behind her her employers had their heads together over a printout.

An old fellow in a quilted fur-collared jacket left the shop just before me, and feeling by now in a busybody mood, I followed him down the market street. I thought he might afford some clues about the incident within—I might find him laughing disagreeably about it with a friend, or alternatively shaking his head in regret. But instead he did something almost stagily French. He walked around the corner at the end of the street, where two open-air pissoirs were fixed to the walls, and relieved himself in silence. I returned to the car and drove on.

Look at this wonderful account of a very ordinary event: a trip to buy toothpaste at the pharmacy. Through description of the shop's setting (*hushed, austerely up-to-date, filing system of gray steel*); the recording of gestures (*deft manipulations of Scotch tape,* the all-important elbow-bump); descriptions of conversations (*in undertones, murmured*); characterizations of people (customers *elderly and well wrapped up,* the *flustered* assistant hastily tidying her hair, the *stony-faced* wife); and inclusion of her own very idiosyncratic responses (*the old stories, the idle little bitch*), we are there inside Morris's story wondering about the motives of this young shop assistant, enjoying with Morris the "almost stagily French" fellow in the fur-collared jacket.

ENCOUNTERS AND OBSERVATIONS

With an eye to detail, dash down notes on serendipitous encounters with people. Include notes on setting, people's physical appearances, etc. Use your senses and jot down your impressions. Record "caught" data such as these:

CHANCE INTERACTIONS

Sketch interactions with: the grocer, the clerk at the kiosk, the travel agent, the woman in the tea shop, the man who helped fix your flat tire . . .

OVERHEARD CONVERSATIONS

Jot down as much of the dialogue as you can.

QUICK OBSERVATIONS

Scribble down descriptions of people seen on the street. Jot down what they are wearing, who they're with, their posture, their gestures . . . Take notes on people working, going to church, arguing, interacting with children . . .

ACTIVITIES

DATE / SETTING	Describe the place in which the activity is taking place.

THE ACTIVITY	Outline the activity being engaged in: the how-to nuts and bolts.

THE SOCIAL ATMOSPHERE

Describe the social scene and atmosphere—
genial, tense, hurried . . .

Take note also of people's attitudes toward
you—jokes, people's interest in you . . .

CONVERSATIONS

Record conversations between
and with people.

NONVERBAL COMMUNICATION

Jot down gestures and unspoken communications you may notice.

YOUR RESPONSE

Make note of your feelings and thoughts as you participated and how they evolved over time.

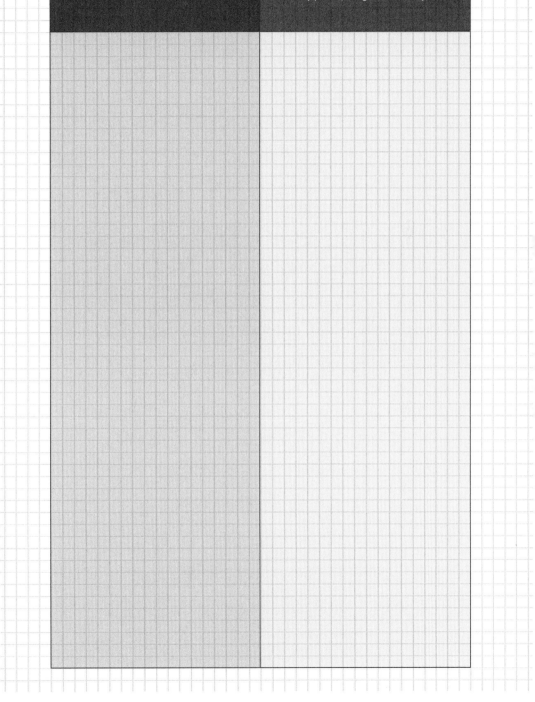

INFORMATION GLEANED

Summarize what you gained or learned by participating in this activity.

FACTS, HISTORY, AND CULTURE

Often forgotten but frequently integral to field notebook-keeping are basic facts, such as the population or geography of the locale in focus and notes on its history and culture.

Snakes and Ladders is Gita Mehta's kaleidoscope of India. Here she puts forth some of the basic facts about her native country:

> To take the obvious contradictions first. Most Indians view other Indians as foreigners, and with considerable justification. The British governed only two-thirds of India. The other third was made up of over five hundred independent kingdoms, so the geography, the races, the languages, the customs of India have less in common than their equivalents among the actually separate nations of Europe or the Americas.
>
> I once asked a man from southern India who was working for an Indian diplomat in London if he felt homesick, being so far from home.
>
> "Not really," the man replied. "I am quite used to being abroad. Before I came to London I was working in Delhi."
>
> It was a reasonable answer. India is the sum of a million worlds enclosed by oceans on three sides, by the mighty Himalayas on the north. Within these boundaries are voluptuous eastern cultures circled by rice fields and western desert kingdoms locked in stone fortifications. Descendents of India's earliest inhabitants occupy the jungles sweeping through her heartland; three-thousand-year-old sacred cities still flourish on the banks of her immense rivers; merchant cultures still grow rich from her ancient ports.
>
> So Delhi may be the capital of the Indian nation, but the people of India see themselves as belonging to an Indian universe defying the vagaries of history. The physical features of

their capital support the logic of this view. Delhi has been the center of at least seven empires, each of whose emperors were addicts of monumental architecture, and even a casual drive through the city forces one to brood on the transience of gloria mundi.

In this graceful passage Mehta imparts a broad sense of India's rich multiplicity and delivers en route information about India's geography, history, and population, punctuating it with a quip that captures a key insight into the culture of her vast and glorious native land.

BASIC FACTS

Record here basic background information
about your spotlit place and its people:

POPULATION (OF CONTINENT, COUNTRY, PROVINCE, TOWN)

GEOGRAPHICAL SIZE (OF COUNTRY, CITY, FARM)

PREDOMINANT EMPLOYMENT(S)

LOCAL INDUSTRIES, BUSINESSES, COMMERCIAL PRODUCTS

AGRICULTURAL ACTIVITIES

YEAR OF FOUNDING AND NAMES OF FOUNDERS

CULTURAL, ETHNIC, CLASS, INCOME, RELIGIOUS COMPOSITION

YEARLY CALENDAR, FESTIVITIES, HOLIDAYS

HISTORY

Make notes on the history, sociology,
and politics of this place:

HISTORICAL OVERVIEW

SIGNIFICANT HISTORICAL FIGURES

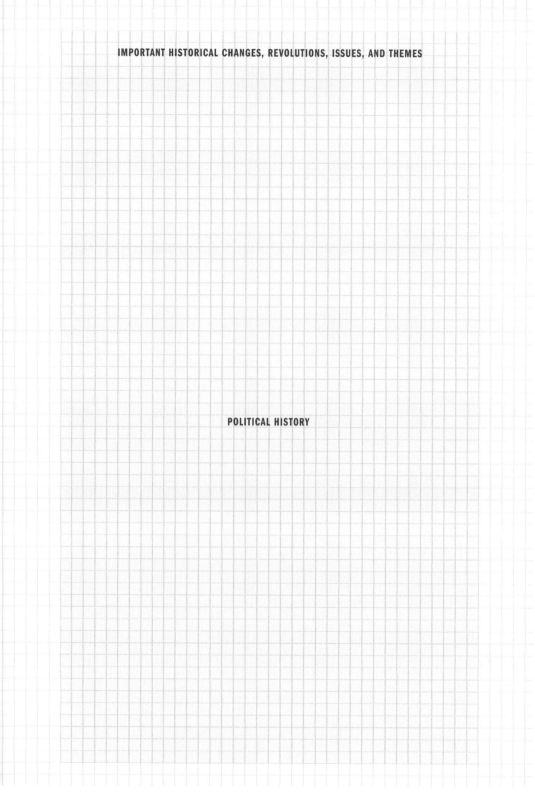

IMPORTANT HISTORICAL CHANGES, REVOLUTIONS, ISSUES, AND THEMES

POLITICAL HISTORY

CURRENT POLITICAL ETHOS AND ISSUES

PROMINENT POLITICIANS

POLITICAL EVENTS THAT OCCUR WHILE YOU'RE THERE

POPULAR FIGURES: INTELLIGENTSIA, FILM STARS, WRITERS, ETC.

CULTURAL OBSERVATIONS

Pen here all sorts of cultural notes. If you are writing about your own culture, view it as would an anthropologist. Range far and wide, jotting down:

LOCAL MAXIMS AND SAYINGS

Note the truisms, aphorisms, and statements of fact expressed by the people you speak with.

GREETINGS

Record how people say hello, good night, and wish each other well.

ACCEPTABLE TOPICS OF CONVERSATION

Notice what people do and don't talk about: Money? Sex? Politics?

EMOTIONS

Register which emotions are expressed openly. Anger, sadness, envy, affection? And note which are not.

STYLE OF DRESS

Portray the various styles of dress— formal and informal.

MANNERS

Make note of the rules of dining etiquette here and the other behaviors that signal good manners.

THE SOUND OF SPEECH

Note the tone of voice people use. Emphatic? Respectful and quiet?

SELF-DEFINITIONS

Dash down what the local people say about themselves as a people, culture, country.

FORMS OF RELAXATION

Depict what people do for fun: music, sports, art, feasts, etc.

SENSE OF WELL-BEING

Note what people take pride in and what they complain about.

WHAT IS LOVED

Log your observations about what people seem to most love.

VALUES

List the most important local values you discern—both those expressed and gleaned. How important are family, work, leisure, friendship, self-development, politics, religion?

MONEY

Compose your impressions of the meaning of money in this place: what it is used to buy, how much is ideal.

POLITICS

Record what people express during political discussions.

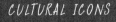
CULTURAL ICONS

Take notes on the people admired, disparaged, and much commented upon by those in this place.

MEDIA

Jot down notes on the stories, people, and behaviors depicted and covered in the local media.

FOOD

Record the meal pattern of this community. Typify what people eat for breakfast, lunch, dinner, tea, etc. Describe delicacies, food presentation, street food, markets and shops, and feasts.

TECHNICAL AND OTHER PERTINENT INFORMATION

To obtain a full picture of the experiences about which you are writing, it may be important to research and make notes in your field notebook about one or more technical processes. If you are doing oral histories with fishermen, you may want to learn netting techniques. If you are remembering your grandmother, you may need to look up her recipe for cornbread. If you are doing watercolors, you may want to research the color ochre.

In this passage from *The Adventures of Tom Sawyer,* Tom Sawyer and Huckleberry Finn are discussing their techniques for curing warts. The excerpt begins with Tom relaying to Huck his spunk-water cure:

"You got to go all by yourself, to the middle of the woods, where you know there's a spunk-water stump, and just as it's midnight you back up against the stump and jam your hand in and say:

'Barley-corn, barley-corn, Injun-meal shorts,

'Spunk-water, spunk-water, swaller these warts,'

And then walk away quick, eleven steps, with your eyes shut, and then turn around three times and walk home without speaking to anybody. Because if you speak the charm's busted."

"Well that sounds like a good way; but that ain't the way Bob Tanner done."

"No sir, you can bet he didn't, becuz he's the wartiest boy in this town; and he wouldn't have a wart on him if he'd knowed how to work spunk-water. I've took thousands of warts off of my hands that way, Huck. I play with frogs so much that I've always got considerable many warts. Sometimes I take em off with a bean."

"Yes, bean's good. I've done that."

"Have you? What's your way?"

"You take and split the bean, and cut the wart so as to get some blood, and then you put the blood on one piece of the bean and take and dig a hole and bury it 'bout midnight at the crossroads in the dark of the moon, and then you burn up the rest of the bean. You see that piece that's got the blood on it will keep drawing and drawing, trying to fetch the other piece to it, and so that helps the blood to draw the wart, and pretty soon off she comes."

"Yes, that's it, Huck—that's it; though when you're burying it, if you say 'Down bean; off wart: come no more to bother me!' it's better."

Although Twain's passage is humorous and fictionalized, he likely took notes on local wart remedies to write this portion of his book. Inclusion of technical and procedural information (scientifically based or grounded in superstition) can greatly enrich written accounts, whether diary, journalism, or fiction, whether for personal or public consumption.

INFORMATIONAL NOTES

Report here the particular ways in which people of this place carry out the various activities, jobs, and processes both directly and indirectly relevant to your interests. Make technical notes here on such activities as:

HOW THEY:

cure warts or hangnails

deliver newspapers

grind wheat

apply pesticides

prepare salad dressing

make school lunches

apply makeup

send messages

manufacture computers

buy railway tickets

wrap oranges

prepare Sunday dinner

gain expertise in their fields

celebrate birthdays

fish for halibut

milk cows

wash clothes

CHRONICLE

The events, social interactions, and ponderings of daily life are staples, and rich fodder, for your field notebook.

Here, in a letter to her dear friend Vita Sackville-West, Virginia Woolf recounts her day. Woolf is on vacation in France:

> Tuesday, 5th April [1927]
> . . . I am writing, with difficulty, on a balcony in the shade. Everything is divided into brilliant yellow and ink black. Clive is seated at a rickety table writing on huge sheets of foolscap, which he picks out from time to time in red ink. This is The history of Civilisation. He has by him Chambers's Dictionary of the English Language. We all sit in complete silence. Underneath, on the next balcony, Vanessa and Duncan are painting the loveliest pictures of rolls of bread, oranges, and wine bottles. In the garden, which is sprinkled with saucers of daisies, red and white, and pansies, the gardener is hoeing the completely dry earth. There is also the Mediterranean—and some bare bald grey mountains, which I look at, roasting in the sun, and think Vita is climbing over hills like that at this moment. I hope your rubber shoes are doing well. Talk of solitude—I think your analysis highly subtle (oh yes and you're a clever donkey West: an original donkey: for all your golden voice, which has the world by the ears). It is the last resort of the civilised: our souls are so creased and soured in meaning we can only unfold them when we are alone. So Leonard thinks; and is determined to buy a farm house here and live alone, with me, half the year. It may be our form of religion. But then what becomes of friendship, love, intimacy? Nessa says, suddenly, she had been wondering why one is supposed to attend to people. Other relations seem to her far more important. I say, that's what Vita says in her letter this morning. Heard from Vita? Says Clive, pricking up his

ears, like a war horse, out at grass—(for he has renounced the world, and puts water in his wine, and looks incredibly pink and fresh). Yes, I say. And off we go, discussing you and Harold and Dottie. . . .

Then Colonel Teed and Miss Campbell came to lunch—he is a retired cavalry officer, she his mistress: both together vine growers, living in a divine 17th Century manor house, set with cypresses, painted, tiled, with tanks of frogs and Roman aqueducts. Miss Campbell was sitting in the dusk silent; and then the frogs began again; and the Colonel made us come in and drink several kinds of wine in his great empty room, and we were given bunches of wild tulips, Vita, and why don't we all live like that, Vita?

In this passage Virginia Woolf brings alive the chance particulars of her life on April 5, 1927. She notes:

The color of the light

A friend's activity: the color of his ink, the table at which he sits, the title of the book he's reading

The subjects of the pictures her sister and partner are painting

The garden flowers and the movements of the gardener

The vista she beholds

The weather and the sensations it arouses on her skin

Her friend's face and attitude

Topics discussed with friends

Luncheon visitors: a reminiscence of a visit to their home, the wine, the flowers

She includes her musings on this particular afternoon: her sense of the necessity of solitude; her hesitations about buying a farm; her yearning for a life where one listens to frogs, drinks wine, and receives tulips.

RECORD OF DAILY ACTIVITIES AND TRAVELS

Record the activities of your daily life, striving for the sensory and factual detail that makes for vivid accounts such as Woolf's.

DATE	Record dates and times of departures and arrivals.

WEATHER	Note weather conditions.

ACTIVITIES

Log the activities of the day, whatever they may be: trips to shops, museums, meetings, visits to and from friends, domestic tasks, etc.

PEOPLE SEEN

Remember who you saw. Describe them with a couple of distinguishing details. Try to capture also the gist of interesting conversations.

MEALS

Record meals eaten at home and elsewhere. Note names of and briefly describe restaurants, bars, cafés.

Make notes about furnishings, lighting, decorations, signs, wait staff, patrons, sounds, smells, energy.

Describe meals, good, bad, and indifferent, and note their cost.

Jot down or obtain a copy of menus (if significant).

TRAVELS

Record lodgings, methods of transport and travel routes.

Note names of campgrounds, hotels, B&Bs.

Describe staff, lobby, rooms, atmosphere, unique features, cost.

Jot down method of transport. Register: vehicle type, rental fees/cost of (train/bus) ticket, price of gas, etc.

Describe: Fellow passengers and interactions

Views out the window

Sights and occurrences along the way

Rest stops

Hitches and mishaps

Note down roads taken
Trace the route on a map

REFLECTIONS

Make note of the topics about which you've mused this day. Comment on your activities and what they made you think and feel.

PERSONAL RESPONSES

The writer's personal emotional responses to the occurrences of his or her life are essential. They may, in fact, be the heart, the main point, the upshot of the field notebook.

Alastair Reid offers his emotional response to arrivals in new cities in *Whereabouts: Notes on Being a Foreigner:*

> I come suddenly into a foreign city, just as the lamps take light along the water, with some notes in my head. Arriving—the mood and excitement, at least, are always the same. I try out the language with the taxi driver, to see if it is still there; and later, I walk to a restaurant that is lurking round a corner in my memory. Nothing, of course, has changed; but cities flow on, like water, and, like water, they close behind any departure. We come back to confirm them, even though they do not particularly care. Or perhaps we come back to confirm ourselves?

Here Reid evokes what it is to arrive in a foreign city to which one has paid previous visits. Through a recounting of his actions (*I try out the language; I walk to a restaurant that is lurking around a corner in my memory*), he awakens in the reader "the mood and excitement" of such arrivals. Via lyrical sentences and use of the simile of flowing water, he arouses, too, the wistfulness of human attachment to places (in the face of their indifference) as well as the need for confirmation. Thus he kindles in the reader a subtle but affecting yearning.

FEELINGS AND CONTEMPLATIONS

Record your emotions and responses to the happenings of each day.

EXPRESS:

How you feel in response to the people and places you've encountered. Do you feel comfortable, anxious, fearful, curious, inspired . . . ?

How this experience compares with experiences you've had in other times and places.

Issues, questions, thoughts, memories aroused by your encounters.

Thoughts about your own development: how you are evolving and your perspectives changing in response to life's offerings.

COMMONPLACE NOTES: PERSPECTIVES OF OTHERS AND MISCELLANEA

The commonplace book, a tradition of note-keeping from fifteenth-century England, is a compendium or scrapbook of notes of any and every kind: medical recipes, quotes, letters, poems, tables of weights and measures, proverbs, prayers, legal formulas. Commonplaces are traditionally used to keep track of useful ideas, bits of wisdom, and facts the possessor doesn't want to forget. Authors such as Hardy and Twain, and others of literary bent, kept common-place books of "literary memoranda"—rough notes and messy jottings from their reading. I encourage you to include in your field notebook a section for commonplacing—for the storage of the perspectives of other writers, thinkers, and such, as well as to catch any and all other sundry tidbits of interest.

Here is the opening to Phillip Lopate's essay "Against Joie de Vivre":

Over the years I have developed a distaste for the spectacle of *joie de vivre*, the knack of knowing how to live. Not that I disapprove of all hearty enjoyment of life. A flushed sense of happiness can overtake a person anywhere, and one is no more to blame for it than the Asiatic flu or a sudden benevolent change in the weather (which is often joy's immediate cause). No, what rankles me is the stylization of this private condition into a bullying social ritual.

The French, who have elevated the picnic to their highest rite, are probably most responsible for promoting this smugly upbeat, flaunting style. It took the French genius for formalizing the informal to bring sticky sacramental sanctity to the baguette, wine, and cheese. A pure image of sleeveless *joie de vivre* Sundays can also be found in Renoir's paintings. Weekend satyrs dance and wink, leisure takes on a Bohemian stripe. A decent writer, Henry

Miller, caught the French malady and ran back to tell us of pissoirs in the Paris streets (why this should have impressed him so, I've never figured out).

But if you want a double dose of *joie de vivre,* you need to consult a later, hence more stylized, version of the French myth of pagan happiness: those Family of Man photographs of endlessly kissing lovers, snapped by Doisneau and Boubat, or Cartier-Bresson's icon of the proud tyke carrying bottles of wine. If Cartier-Bresson and his disciples are excellent photographers for all that, it is in spite of their occasionally rubbing our noses in a tediously problematic "affirmation of life."

In this contrarian personal essay, Lopate harvests his commonplace book (mental or tangible) of notations on works and perspectives of other artists and writers. He brings to bear Renoir, Miller, Doisneau, and others in his rumination about the flaws of showily hearty living—and enriches his own work thereby.

QUOTATIONS AND THOUGHTS
FROM EXPERTS, SCHOLARS,
AND LITERARY FOREBEARS—
AND OTHER MISCELLANEA

ARCHIVE HERE,
IN THE TRADITION OF THE
COMMONPLACE BOOK:

Perspectives of experts on
pertinent issues.

Thoughts of scholars about this place,
its history, geography, and culture.

Quotes from classical writings.

Passages from other contemporary
writers that interest you or are
pertinent to the focus of
your field notebook.

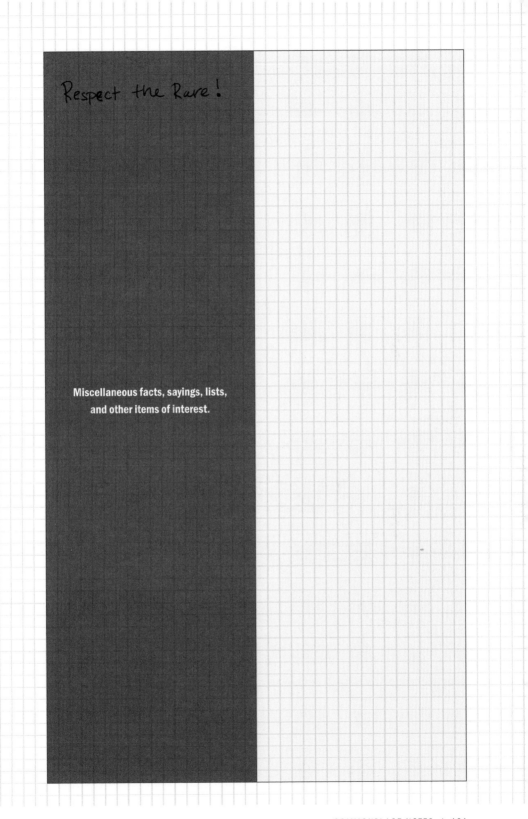

Respect the Rare!

**Miscellaneous facts, sayings, lists,
and other items of interest.**

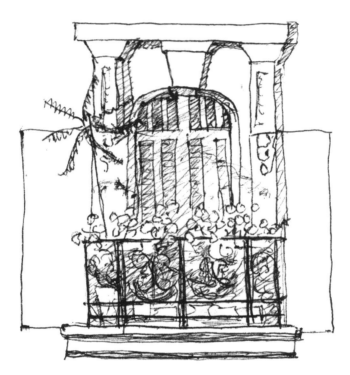

ASSOCIATIONS AND FIGURATIVE LANGUAGE

In your notebook, charge your imagination to conjure fresh direct and indirect comparisons that will shock the reader into new ways of perceiving the world. Simile and metaphor are playful, versatile tools for making places and people bustle and cluck like farmyard chickens and your reflections and experiences cool, glinting ponds on the page.

METAPHOR AND SIMILE

W. G. Sebald ponders here the remnants of the pre–World War I windmills he came across during the long ramble through Suffolk he recounts in his book *The Rings of Saturn.* Readers are thus afforded the pleasure of the unique visual association supplied by his drifting mind:

> I was once told by someone who could remember the turning sails in his childhood, that the white flecks of the windmills lit up the landscape just as a tiny highlight brings light to a painted eye.

In *Black Lamb and Grey Falcon: A Journey through Yugoslavia,* Rebecca West enticingly compares the color of a Dalmatian town to a variety of baked goods:

> Across a milk-white sea, with two silver hydroplanes soaring and dipping to our right and left, we came to the town of Trogir. . . . It is one of those golden-brown cities: the colour of rich crumbling shortbread, of butterscotch, of the best pastry.

In her memoir, *A Cross and a Star: Memoirs of a Jewish Girl in Chile,* Marjorie Agosin recalls, through various felicitous metaphors, a bountiful woman who worked for her Aunt Luisa:

> There was something unusual about Etelvina; as soon as she arrived anywhere the wilted geraniums would bloom, the wheat flour would raise [sic] proudly, the obstructed pipes would unclog and

whistle more than ever before, and the house would fill up with beautiful and strange individuals. . . . Everyone came to Luisa's house so that Etelvina could cure them with her mountain-like eyes and her watermelon heart.

W. Somerset Maugham responds, rhapsodically, via a resounding metaphor, to the color of the Sarawak jungle in his journal *A Writer's Notebook:*

> A green hill. The jungle reached to its crest, an intoxication of verdure, and the luxuriousness was such that it left you breathless and embarrassed. It was a symphony of green, as though a composer working in colour instead of with sound had sought to express something extraordinarily subtle in a barbaric medium. The greens ranged from the pallor of the aquamarine to the profundity of jade. There was an emerald that blared like a trumpet and a pale sage that trembled like a flute.

Charles Dickens, in his fictional masterpiece *Great Expectations,* offers us a certain Mr. Wemmick, whose face he likens to a block of wood carved by a carpenter:

> Casting my eyes on Mr. Wemmick . . . I found him to be a dry man, rather short in stature, with a square wooden face, whose expression seemed to have been imperfectly chipped out with a dull-edged chisel. There were some marks in it that might have been

dimples if the material had been softer and the instrument finer, but which, as it was, were only dints.

In *I Know Why the Caged Bird Sings* memoirist Maya Angelou conveys, via a delicious metaphor that craftily both whets our appetites and makes us gulp, the bigotry that prevailed in certain segregated American towns:

> People in Stamps used to say that the whites in our town were so prejudiced that a Negro couldn't buy vanilla ice cream. Except on July Fourth. Other days he had to be satisfied with chocolate.

Naturalist and paleontologist George Gaylord Simpson describes here, in his 1934 volume *Attending Marvels: A Patagonian Journal*, the recalcitrant armadillo named Florrie, whom Simpson attempted to tame:

> With our tender hearts, we gave her an old sack to sleep under and the ungrateful wretch piled it in a corner of her box, climbed over it, and hit for the open spaces. . . . Her only reaction to our most friendly advances was suddenly to uncurl, emitting at the same time an explosive wheeze, a very startling maneuver like having a mild cigar explode in one's face.

Michael Ondaatje seduces the reader into feeling the power of the Ceylonese heat by way of a wonderfully viscid simile in his memoir of his Sri Lanka childhood, *Running in the Family:*

> We are back within the heat of Colombo, in the hottest month of the year. It is delicious heat. Sweat runs with its own tangible life down the body as if a giant egg has been broken onto our shoulders.

In his *American Notebooks,* Nathaniel Hawthorne offers a delightfully humble vegetable simile to name the happiness he would feel if he could be granted just one carefree day. The modest self-regard of the great writer should inspire all aspiring notebook keepers to forge humbly on, whether squashes or not:

> Friday, June 23d.—Summer has come at last—the longest days, with blazing sunshine, and fervid heat. . . . Could I only have the freedom to be perfectly idle now,—no duty to fulfill, no mental or physical labor to perform,—I should be as happy as a squash, and much in the same mode; but the necessity of keeping my brain at work eats into my comfort, as the squash-bugs do into the heart of the vines. I keep myself uneasy and produce little, and almost nothing that is worth producing.

METAPHOR AND SIMILE

A landscape dotted with eyes, a town like butterscotch, a woman with a watermelon heart who can make flour rise, a green symphony of a hill, a chisel-chipped face, a town where even the ice cream is bigoted, a cigar-breathing armadillo, eggy sweat, and squash-happiness—all are lively and unforgettable evocations of the writer's experience.

TRY FOR SOME EQUALLY SURPRISING, VISCERAL, AND EVOCATIVE METAPHORS AND SIMILES AS YOU DESCRIBE IN YOUR NOTEBOOK:

Chance Particulars—sense impressions and concrete details.

Places—from landscapes and fauna to towns.

People—portraits, interactions, and encounters.

Historical facts and cultural impressions.

Technical information.

A chronicle of daily life.

Personal responses.

Commonplace notes and miscellanea.

Reflections, thoughts, and musings.

REFLECTIONS

In her classic essay "Seeing," Annie Dillard offers up reflections on the nature of life, taking advantage of the philosophical turn of her well-stocked mind:

When I was six or seven years old, growing up in Pittsburgh, I used to take a precious penny of my own and hide it for someone else to find. It was a curious compulsion; sadly, I've never been seized by it since. For some reason I always "hid" the penny along the same stretch of sidewalk up the street. I would cradle it at the roots of a sycamore, say, or in a hole left by a chipped-off piece of sidewalk. Then I would take a piece of chalk, and, starting at either end of the block, draw huge arrows leading up to the penny from both directions. After I learned to write I labeled the arrows: SURPRISE AHEAD or MONEY THIS WAY. I was greatly excited, during all this arrow-drawing, at the thought of the first lucky passer-by who would receive in this way, regardless of merit, a free gift from the universe. But I never lurked about. I would go straight home and not give the matter another thought, until, some months later, I would be gripped again by the impulse to hide another penny.

It is still the first week in January, and I've got great plans. I've been thinking about seeing. There are lots of things to see, unwrapped gifts and free surprises. The world is fairly studded and strewn with pennies cast broadside from a generous hand. But—and this is the point—who gets excited by a mere penny? If you follow one arrow, if you , crouch motionless on a bank to watch a tremulous ripple thrill on the water and are rewarded by a muskrat kit paddling from its den, will you count that sight a chip of copper only, and go your rueful way? It is dire poverty indeed when a man is so malnourished and fatigued that he won't stoop to pick up a penny. But if you cultivate a healthy poverty and simplicity, so that finding a penny will literally make your day, then, since the world is in fact planted in pennies, you have with your poverty bought a lifetime of days. It is that simple. What you see is what you get.

Dillard gives free play to her recipe for a good life, using the sighting of muskrats and the discovery of dropped pennies as metaphors and props in her view that cultivating a spirit of simplicity and, most particularly, grabbing what you see make for daily pleasure.

THOUGHTS AND MUSINGS

Allow yourself to philosophize and wonder on the page. By expressing these ponderings, you ensure that your field notebook will contain, and that you will be able to offer a reader, a great gift: your wisdom. Looking always for contrasts, contradictions, and ironies, and for complex, dual, and multiple truths . . .

CHRONICLE HERE:

Questions, Hunches, and Musings

Reflections, Analyses, and Insights

Generalizations and Hypotheses

Philosophical Ruminations

WRITING NOTES

KEEP HERE IDEAS FOR MORE
FORMAL WRITING THAT MAY
BE ASSEMBLED FROM THESE
NOTES, IDEAS ON SUCH
ELEMENTS AS:

Genre: memoir, article, novel,
essay, poetry, blog, etc.

The story, main idea, central question.

Themes.

Story structure: narrative arc,
plot, driving line.

The beginning.

Building blocks and anchors:
types of passages, central metaphor,
key images, takeaway wisdom.

Balance of scenes, narrative,
and reflection.

Principal encounters,
people, characters.

Pivotal moments, scenes,
emotional beats.

Key insights or findings
or contentions.

Voice, persona, and point of view.

Time: retrospective/immediate lens,
past/present tense.

Sense of place.

Chance particulars: vital
concrete and sensory details.

Perspectives of others
to be summoned.

History, cultural observations, facts,
and miscellanea to include.

The ending.

ACKNOWLEDGMENTS

Cheese and chocolates and spring showers of thanks to:

The various authors cited herein, who afforded me both pleasure and inspiration, and whose elegant passages, I hope, will inspire readers of *Chance Particulars* to seize and savor their full works.

Elizabeth Demers—my brilliant, consummate editor—and all the others at Johns Hopkins University Press who welcomed and cheered on this unexpected chance of a book.

The many talented and warmhearted students who taught me—along with my own stumbling attempts at worldscribing—what particulars ought to be contained in its pages.

My generous and wonderful daughter, Maud, who stretched herself to use pen, rather than her preferred charcoals and oil paints, and create lovely illustrations to accompany her mother's words.

And literary master Thomas Mallon, for the delightful phrase that snagged on some rogue fishhook in my brain and became the title of this book.

APPENDIX

NOTES TO TAKE ON THE WORLD: A QUICK REFERENCE

Sensory data
- smells
- sounds
- sights
- textures
- tastes

History and facts
- population
- businesses
- farm products
- social groups
- history
- politics
- culture

Responses and reflections
- personal responses
- thoughts and reflections

Commonplace notes
- quotations
- miscellanea

Associations
- metaphors and similes

Daily chronicle
- date
- weather
- activities
  - setting
  - conversation
  - people
  - atmosphere
  - process
- meals
- travels, transport, and route
- mishaps

Place
- towns
  - layout
  - shops
  - public buildings
  - restaurants
  - street scenes
  - signs
  - pace
- architecture
- interior settings
- landscape
- flora and fauna

Items to collect
- maps
- ticket stubs
- brochures
- ads
- newspapers and magazines
- articles
- menus
- handouts

People
- people
  - physical appearance
  - gestures
  - voice
  - habits
  - possessions
  - dreams
- overheard conversations
- chance encounters
  - kiosk
  - grocer
  - gas station
- quick observations
  - people on street
  - in cafes
- interviews
  - setting
  - activities
  - tone
  - key quotes
  - gist
  - technical info (e.g., cutting bread, curing warts)
- cultural observations
  - sayings
  - conversation topics
  - dress
  - rules of decorum
  - values

Sara Mansfield Taber is a writer of several forms of literary nonfiction: personal essays, memoirs, and portraits of people and places. She is the author of *Born Under an Assumed Name: The Memoir of a Cold War Spy's Daughter*, winner of the Foreword Reviews 2012 Silver Medal for autobiography and memoir. She has also published two books of literary journalism: *Dusk on the Campo: A Journey in Patagonia* and *Bread of Three Rivers: The Story of a French Loaf.* Her short essays, reviews, and political commentary have been published in literary magazines and newspapers such as *The American Scholar* and the *Washington Post* and produced for public radio. She is a past recipient of a William Sloane Fellowship in Nonfiction for the Bread Loaf Writer's Conference and has been awarded several residencies at the Virginia Center for the Creative Arts. A long-time instructor at The Writer's Center in Bethesda, Maryland, she has also taught in the Master of Arts in Writing program at Johns Hopkins University and the Vermont College of Fine Arts as well as in seminars across the United States and abroad.

Taber was raised in Asia, Europe, and the United States, the daughter of a covert CIA officer. She has a BA from Carleton College, an MSW from the University of Washington, and a doctorate from Harvard University, where she specialized in cross-cultural human development, a blend of psychology and anthropology. A former field biologist, psychiatric social worker, and professor of social work, she has published scholarly works in the social and biological sciences and been the recipient of many scholarly grants and fellowships, including a Spencer Foundation fellowship from the National Academy of Education. Her studies of adolescence across cultures and of Mexican and Vietnamese immigrants, as well as the inquiries she has made into the lives of Spanish villagers, Argentine sheep ranchers, and French bread bakers as a literary journalist, have made her an appassionato of and an expert on the field notebook.

ABOUT THE ARTIST

Maud Taber-Thomas is an artist who
specializes in oil paintings and charcoal
drawings. Trained in classical techniques
at the New York Academy of Art, and
with a background in English literature from Bowdoin College and Oxford
University, Maud Taber-Thomas draws
inspiration for her evocative portraits,
interiors, and landscapes from the narra-
tives and characters of classic literature.
Her works, which range in scale from
miniature to larger than life, capture the
vibrant light and color of far-off places
and distant time periods. Maud Taber-
Thomas lives in Takoma Park, Maryland,
and teaches drawing and painting
classes at the National Gallery of Art
and the Yellow Barn Studio at Glen Echo.
Her drawings and paintings have been
shown at a number of galleries in the
Washington, DC, area and in New York.
Her work is represented by Susan
Calloway Fine Arts, in Washington, DC,
and can be viewed on her website,
Maudtaber-thomas.com.

Here before me now is my picture, my map, of a
place and therefore of myself, and much that can never
be said adds to its reality for me, just as much of its
reality is based on my own shadows, my inventions.

–M. F. K. Fisher

NOTES

NOTES

NOTES

NOTES

NOTES

NOTES

NOTES

NOTES